ROCKHOUSE / STRANG ARCHITECTURE

AN OPEN TERRACE FLOA

ING BETWEEN TREETOPS

ROCKHOUSE / STRANG ARCHITECTURE

TEXT BY **BYRON HAWES** | EPILOGUE BY **MAX STRANG**
PRINCIPAL PHOTOGRAPHY BY **CLAUDIO MANZONI**

OSCAR RIERA OJEDA
PUBLISHERS

CONTENTS

INTRODUCTION
BY BYRON HAWES

ROCKHOUSE
MIAMI, FLORIDA

'I call architecture frozen music.' -Johann Wolfgang von Goethe

Though, practically, a utilitarian reference to the universal theme of expression underscoring all creative disciplines, Goethe's statement functions as a markedly intuitive method of examining architecture. Because, of course, as with other creative métiers, architecture is divided into markedly different thematic genres, which see great corollary with music.

The icy tones and crystalline intellectualism of Philip Glass emblematic of the emotional isolationism of the modernists; the cyberpunk dystopian futurism of Kid A-era Radiohead evocative of the post-structural curvilinearity of Zaha Hadid and the fluids.

Max Strang's wondrous RockHouse, however, is something else. Something warm and luxurious; full of delicacy and depth. Fado sung softly on the beach in Estoril. Flamenco guitar by candlelight on the boardwalk in Donostia. Palm fronds dancing in the wind.

Our relationship to both architecture and music differ from the way we interact with other artforms. We find ourselves awash in them; foundering less purely emotive interactions than overarching envelopments of harmonic design. Extra-sensorial experiences with great capability to impact us in tangible ways.

Residential Interpretations
From a philosophical perspective, residential architecture occupies a unique position amongst design pursuits. More than any other form of building, the residence imbues itself into the very fibre of its owner's being.

Architecture has the power to dramatically impose itself upon its utilizers. A well-programmed office fosters productivity. A well laid-out restaurant allows ease and efficiency. But residential architecture must transcend both form and function, even while embodying them both. It must be interactive, practicable, and comfortable; anticipating the needs and lifestyle of its residents.

Brancusi may have referred to architecture as 'inhabited sculpture', but edifices such as the RockHouse differs. Despite the aesthetic qualities, this is first and foremost a vehicle for living; an experiential entity crafted with a specific lifestyle modality in mind.

Landscape
Many architects believe that 'reading' the site of a given building is of crucial importance. That landscape and environment must not only sustain a project, but inspire it. That a symbiosis between building and environment is paramount, and that the structure can and must become a part of its landscape.

Max Strang has spoken at length about his inspirations for this project. In a recent interview he discussed the essential motivations behind the unique style of RockHouse. To wit: 'Here, a lot of people have houses like air-conditioned boxes. We wanted to enjoy the climate and outdoor living. The house is a bit like a tree cabin and was inspired by some of the houses we saw on Bali. We translated that approach into the here and now. After all, it is a kind of jungle here, at least that's what it feels like with the profusion of greenery all around.'

RockHouse is based in the Southern Miami neighbourhood of Coconut Grove, a veritable subtropical jungle. Palm trees, Mangrove,

RockHouse south elevation (opposite page); Geoffrey Bawa's Villa Batujimbar in Bali, Indonesia (top); Gene Leedy's Architect Strang Residence in Winter Haven, Florida, 1970 (above).

The roof of the RockHouse echoes Gene Leedy's Dormon Residence, built in Winter Haven, Florida, in 1963. Photograph by Gene Leedy Architect (above).

Royal Poincianas, and Strangler Figs intermingle in a symphony of luscious greenery. Directly across the street is the noted horticulturalist and plant collector David Fairchild's iconic Kampong compound, which is now the National Tropical Botanical Garden.

Using Coconut Grove's sprawling vegetation as an aesthetic jumping-off point, Strang has reinterpreted the South Florida area's lushness and tropicality in the manner of warm weather vernacular architecture's spiritual home: Southeast Asia.

This manner of architecture isn't distinguished simply by aesthetic properties, but also by a lifestyle it espouses. A rejection of the compartmentalization of indoor and outdoor spaces; an appreciation of, and interaction with, its surroundings. A direct relationship with nature.

Lessons of Vernacularity
Luis Barragán once said that 'Any work of architecture which does not express serenity is a mistake'; a crystal clear expression of the essential tenets of tropical architecture.

While traditional Balinese residences are typically built as a series of distinct pavilions, surrounding a central courtyard, the RockHouse is structurally more in keeping with the classic structure of the island of Borneo; the Longhouse. Longhouses, in their original form, are

long, proportionately narrow buildings, with one side delineated into distinct social or living spaces by virtue of interior design, and the other divided into private living quarters.

The design of RockHouse is a refined amalgamation of elements of both longhouses and the discussed Balinese compounds.

The ground floor is laid out more or less as a single long structure, with one side occupied by large kitchen/dining rooms and a living room. These are separated by a staircase, concealed on both ends by storage spaces. The other side is comprised entirely of the master suite, incorporating bedroom, bathroom, closet, and WC. On the eastern elevation the structure juts outwards, giving space for two additional bedrooms.

The first floor comprises nearly entirely of terrace spaces, clad in ipe wood decking. On opposing sides there is an enclosed den space, and a fourth bedroom. These are surrounded by outdoor living, dining, and kitchen spaces. The entire floor is protected by wood and steel railings at the exterior, and shielded from above by a flat roof of industrial steel, which functions as an umbrella, sheltering the house.

By combining the open internal structural elements of longhouses on the family's ground floor living and private spaces with the indoor/out-

Courtyard of the Strang Residence features exposed structural elements, Gene Leedy Architect, Winter Haven, Florida, 1970. Photograph by Max Strang (above).

door coalescence of Balinese compound architecture on the first floor, Strang has rather ingeniously expanded the purview of tropical living. The ground floor is specifically designed to commune with nature; with myriad terrace doors opening to the grounds. The house itself is 24 feet wide, and is designed in such a way that inhabitants are never more than 12 feet from a door or window, furthering that sense of the continuity of indoor and outdoor spaces. In an era of indoor living, dominated by small screens, RockHouse gently guides its inhabitants out of doors, constantly framing the simple sublimity of the sunset just outside.

The first floor functions as a sort of high-concept treehouse, nestled below a wide, flat, overhanging roof. The extended eaves, a hallmark of vernacular architecture, provide shade from the South Floridian sun, while allowing unfettered access to the sub-tropical vistas and gardens beyond.

On the western elevation, a geometric, zig-zagging swimming pool sits in the foundation of a smaller house that was originally on the property. Surrounded by lush vegetation, and centred around a sprawling banana tree, the pool area is a study in naturalized landscape architecture. Stone terraces of variegated elevations connect the pool, hot tub, and seating areas, wholly interspersed with the gardens and sheltered by the tree canopies and overgrowth along the property's perimeters, creating a tranquil respite.

The overall effect is transporting, a tropical villa that feels lightyears removed from its suburban location. A culmination of the ecologically-forward architecture that has defined Strang's career, the tropical architecture that influenced him on his travels, and the Floridian design scene's expansive history of landscape architecture, as seen in the work of the likes of Mario Nievera.

Genesis of an Architect

Architecture has been a vital part of Max Strang's life since an early age. He grew up in a house designed by the noted 'Sarasota School' architect Gene Leedy, who happened to be the father of his closest childhood friend. Many youthful days were spent tagging along to build sites, inspiring a love of design that only fully manifested years later.

After graduation Strang went back to Winter Haven, FL to work for his childhood motivator, before stints in New York at SHoP Architects and Zaha Hadid. The lessons of these experiences remain essential to Strang's work to this day. From SHoP, a unique perspective on modularity in architectural design. From Hadid, an intuitive geospatial fluidity. But the lessons of Sarasota Modern, and Leedy himself, resonate most. Sarasota Modern is oft defined by its warm-weather mid-century characteristics, and its ongoing use of louvers or sunshades, floating staircases, and repeating jalousie windows. However, the central tenets, and true importance, of the movement is in its steadfast adherence

Solomon Residence, Siesta Key, Gene Leedy Architect, 1970. Photograph by Gene Leedy (top left); Paul Rudolph's Martin Harkavy House, Lido Shores, Sarasota, Florida, 1957-1958. Photographs by ESTO (right, top & above); Gene Leedy's Max Strang childhood home, Winter Haven, Florida, 1970. Photograph by Alexander Georges (above left).

to incorporating the topography and characteristics of a site into the larger design of a building; creating a vital connection between architecture and environment.

Inspiration

RockHouse was Strang's first major project at his eponymous firm, and, while its Balinese aesthetics are anomalous in his broader oeuvre, the lessons of warm-weather modernism and creating correlations between indoor and outdoor spaces remain constant.

From a strictly aesthetic perspective, RockHouse is most reminiscent of the great Sri Lankan architect Geoffrey Bawa, a driving force behind tropical modernist architecture (or vernacular architecture), a design movement in which sensitivity for local context is combined with modernist principles of form.

We see in RockHouse echoes of Bawa's Ena de Silva House, with its juxtaposition between the open floor plans and minimalist interior decoration of the Corbusians with iconic elements of South Asian courtyard houses, and his iconic Bentota Beach Hotel, with its overhanging roof and stone walls. Like Bawa, Strang prioritizes natural and local materials. He makes great use of oolitic limestone, which he compounds with fossilized remnants of coral found on-site. Polished concrete, ipe wood, and stone accents are used throughout the interior, creating a rich earthy palette of surfaces and textures. As with Bentota, myriad windows and terrace doors link the in and

out of doors, creating the sensation of garden spaces less adjacent than interstitial.

As mentioned, the Sarasota School of modern architecture has played a major influence on Strang's work. While highly inspired by the philosophies of the Bauhaus, the movement incorporated forms of regional architecture and Florida's macro climate, using patios, terraces, modular construction, and raised floors to effectively open up buildings and provide for greater ventilation. The style also focussed heavily on light and shadow, using brise-soleil, louvers, screens, and cantilevering to create an experiential harmony between indoor and outdoor spaces.

RockHouse incorporates these strategies, albeit through the aesthetic lens of tropical modernism, with the combination of the wide, low-slung roof and the canopy of tree-tops providing a distinct interplay between light and shadow, in a cheeky environmental ode to Paul Rudolph's immortal Umbrella House. The influence of Rudolph's magnum-opus is further evident in RockHouse's almost temple-like quality, and its high roof over the lower building masses allowing for increased cooling and shading. Ground floor windows and doors exist on both long sides of the house, allowing for lateral air circulation. Another major influence is Pierre Koenig's Stahl House; a part of Arts & Architecture magazine's Case Study Program, which aimed to both advance residential architectural aesthetics, but also explore and expand ways of living in, and interacting with, contemporary houses.

Pierre Koenig's Case Study House #22, Los Angeles, California, 1958 (above); Paul Rudolph's Umbrella House in Sarasota, Florida, 1954, features a protective roof covering. Photograph by Library of Congress (below).

The spatial layout of Koenig's tour de force was delineated into public and private aspects, all the while remaining true to the modernist principles of open-plan layouts. The RockHouse echoes this juxtaposition of flow, organization, and program, creating pockets of private space at the axes, while retaining an overarching open concept.

Epilogue

It has often been said that writing about music is like dancing about architecture. But some architecture manifests as music in and of itself. Crooning softly its siren song; whispering in the willows.

Max Strang's RockHouse is just such a building. A masterpiece of interpretive design, amalgamating the ethos' of vernacular architecture and mid-century modernism to create something entirely new.

May 2017

DESIGN

DESCRIPTION

Coconut Grove, just south of Miami's downtown core, is a veritable subtropical jungle. Rolling mangroves spread inland from the beaches along Biscayne Bay. Old Strangler figs ensconce the roads like verdant, vegetative tunnels. The houses are camouflaged by greenery; sheathed in a hammock of leaves and light. It's home to The Kampong, a 9-acre tropical botanical garden that was formerly the winter residence of the famed horticulturalist Dr. David Fairchild, who introduced nearly 30,000 plant species and varietals from across the globe to the United States, and created a garden on the property to contain and display many of the plants that he obtained through his travels. The Grove, as it's affectionately known, is one of the greenest suburban areas in the country.

Across the street from The Kampong is another masterwork; Max Strang's RockHouse. A substantial, rectangular structure set deep on its property, surrounded by a cornucopia of Poincianas and Palms. From afar, only the first floor is visible, a low-slung open terrace of 3400sq/f sheltered by a flat roof and extended trusses, seemingly dancing in the treetops. At a distance, it gives the impression of being entirely separate from any other structure, floating ethereally in the overgrowth.

Designed according to the structural principles of traditional South Asian 'Long Houses', the RockHouse exhibits the lifestyle tenets of tropical modernism, espousing the conflation of indoor and outdoor spaces.

As Strang himself says: 'The basic idea was to have a long house with high ceilings. We wanted to regulate the indoor climate by means of cross ventilation. The width is 24 feet (around 7 metres), so you're never further than 12 feet from a window or door, all of which can be opened. The house was designed from the top downwards. We wanted to live upstairs among the treetops. The roof serves as an umbrella sheltering the whole house'.

The house's ground floor is occupied by familial living spaces. At one end is a spacious living room, dotted with dark ebony-framed windows, giving the impressions of bringing the gardens inside. Next to the living room are the kitchen and dining areas, and in the centre are children's bedrooms, a small office, and washrooms. The other side of the ground floor is given over entirely to the master suite, encompassing a large bedroom, walk-in closet, and master bath. Continuing with the open plan, the bedroom is shielded from the rest of the suite by the bath, which acts as a half-wall directly behind the bed, cloaked in ebony mahogany and Florida Keystone.

A polished concrete floor runs the breadth of the ground floor, further accentuating the open plan continuity, and it is furnished with an eclectic mixture of Balinese-influenced pieces and modern classics from the likes of Marcel Breuer and George Nelson.

The first floor is geared entirely towards outdoor living, with a sweeping terrace of nearly 3400sq/f, encompassing bars, changing rooms, and an outdoor kitchen. The wide, flat roof provides shade and diffuses the searing Floridian sun, as gentle breezes flow across the terrace.

The RockHouse is a statement of outdoor living, but also of that Sarasota Modernist belief in site-specific architecture. The house and grounds were conceptualized simultaneously, which is plainly evident in experiencing the house. The seemingly endless supply of terrace doors and windows allow the interior and exterior spaces to form a symbiotic whole, and the eastern elevation is comprised of rolling outdoor spaces, gardens, and a swimming pool, combining lush greenery and local stone paths and seating areas in various elevations.

The RockHouse has been pivotal in Strang garnering numerous awards, including the AIA Florida Merit Award of Excellence, AIA Miami Young Architect of the Year, and an invitation to the AIA College of Fellows.

SKETCHES

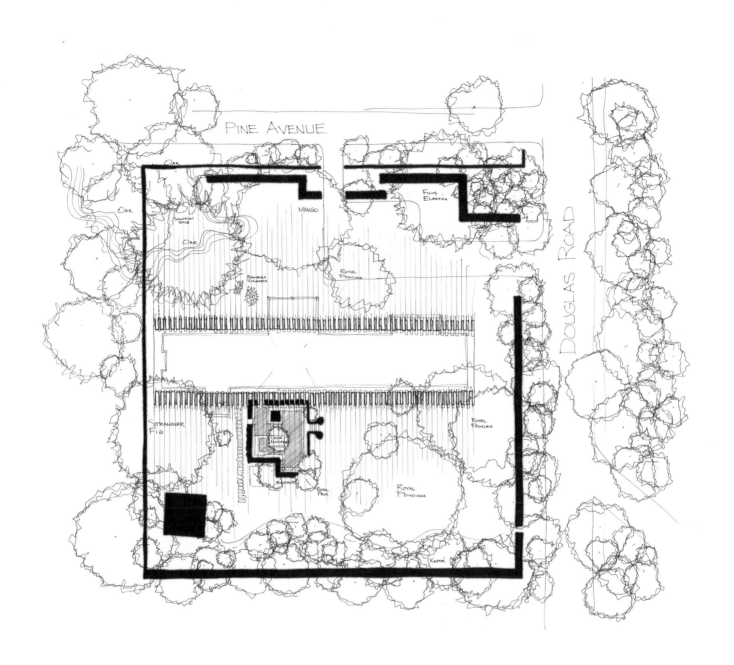

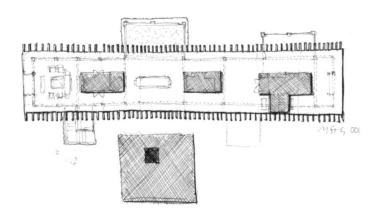

Site and house sketches

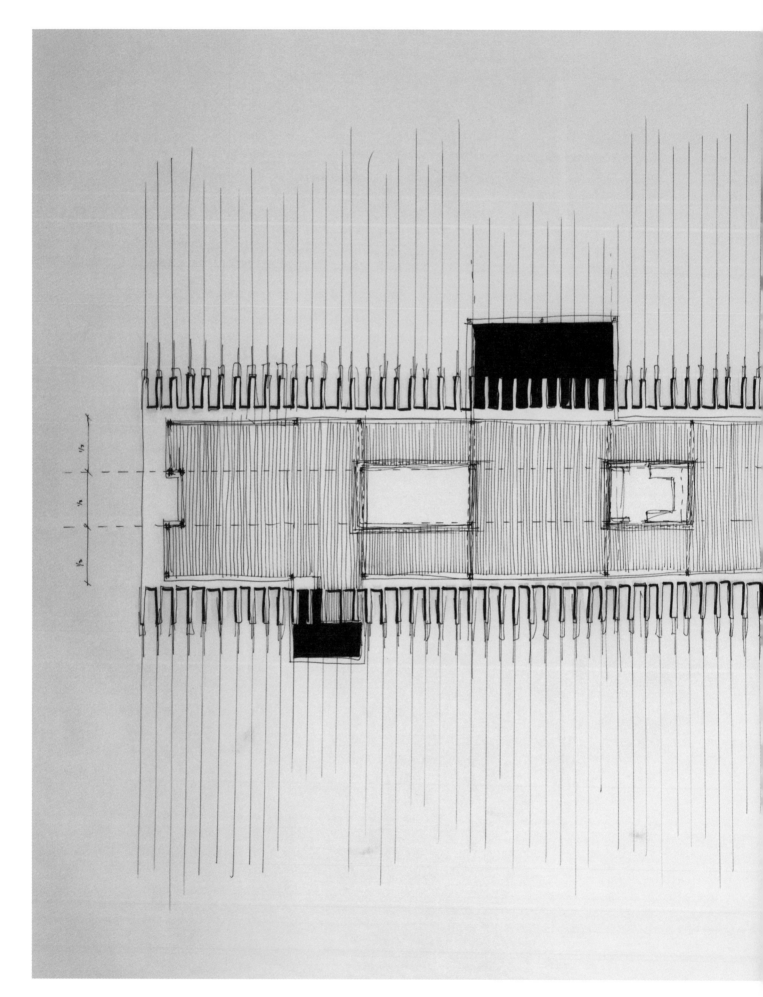

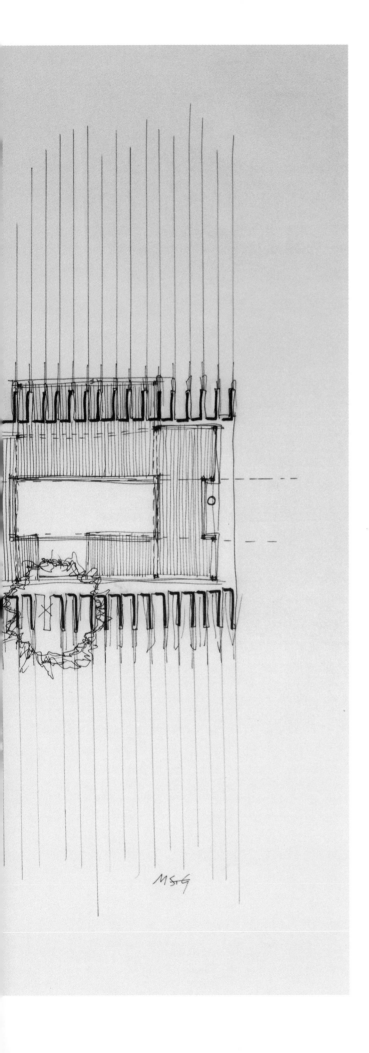

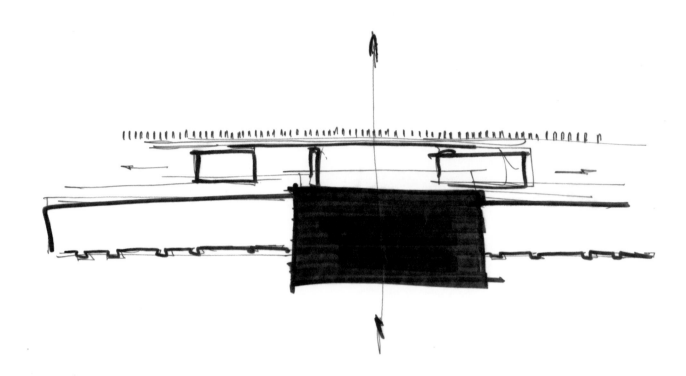

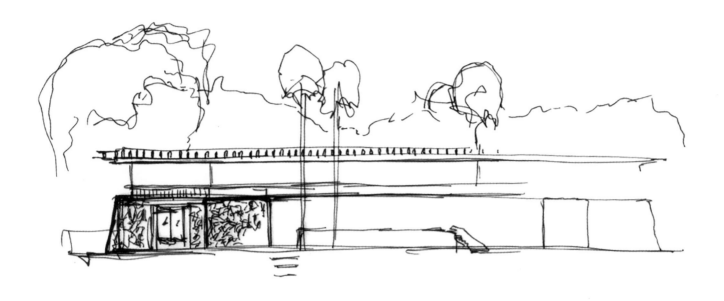

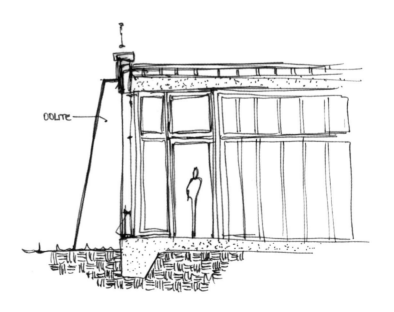

OOLITE

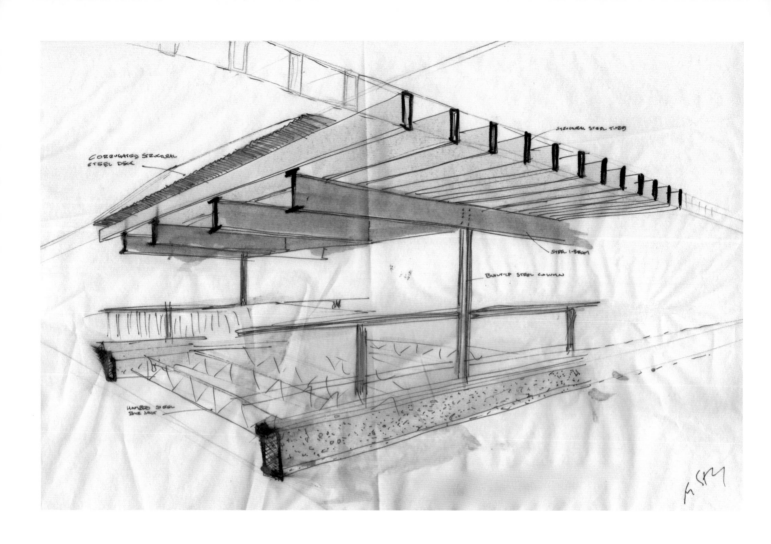

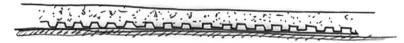

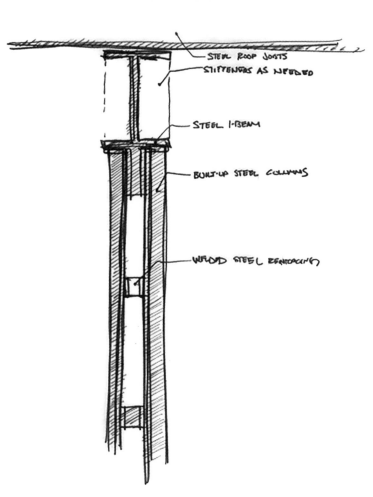

STEEL ROOF JOISTS

STIFFENERS AS NEEDED

STEEL I-BEAM

BUILT-UP STEEL COLUMNS

WELDED STEEL REINFORCING

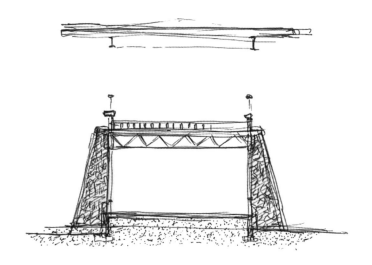

PRESENTATION DRAWINGS

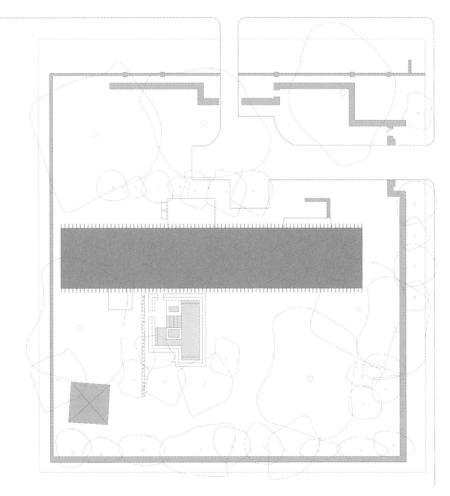

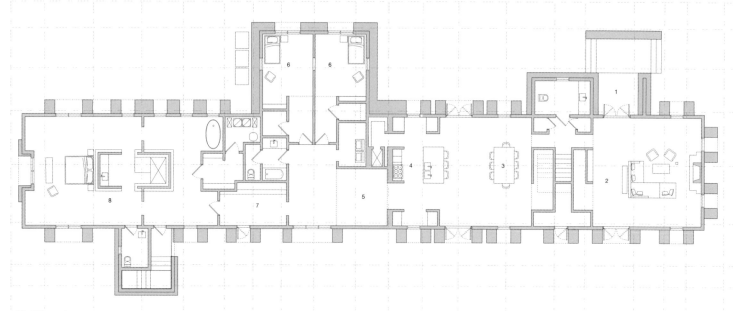

First floor plan

Legend
1. Entry
2. Living
3. Dining
4. Kitchen
5. Den
6. Bedroom
7. Office
8. Master Suite
9. Outdoor Living
10. Outdoor Dining
11. Outdoor Kitchen

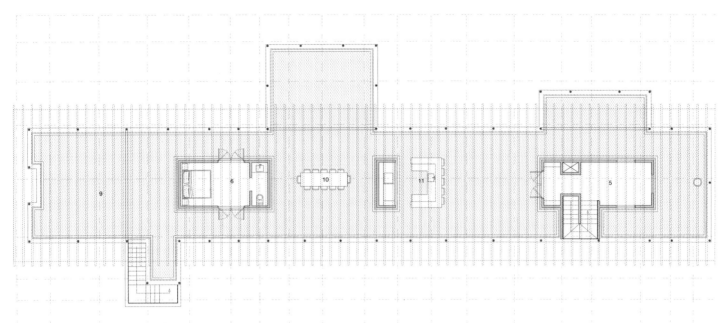

Terrace level plan

North elevation

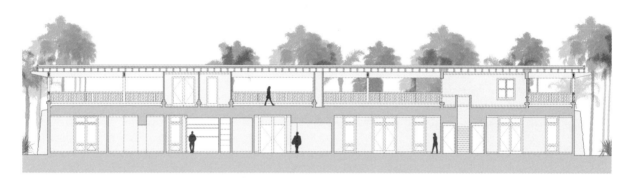

Longitudinal section looking north

South elevation

Cross section looking west

East elevation

Cross section looking east

Cross section looking west

West elevation

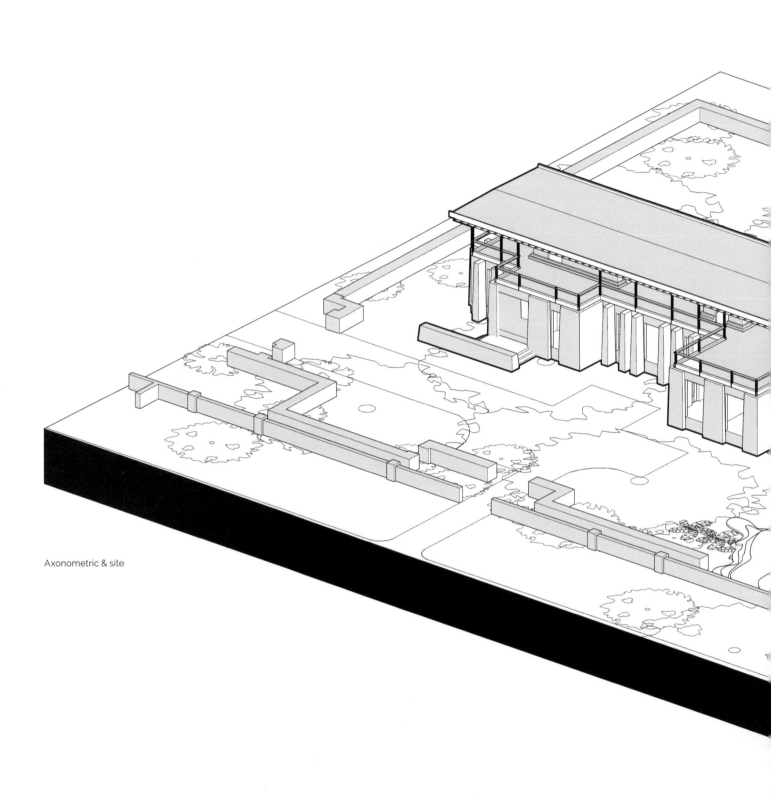

Axonometric & site

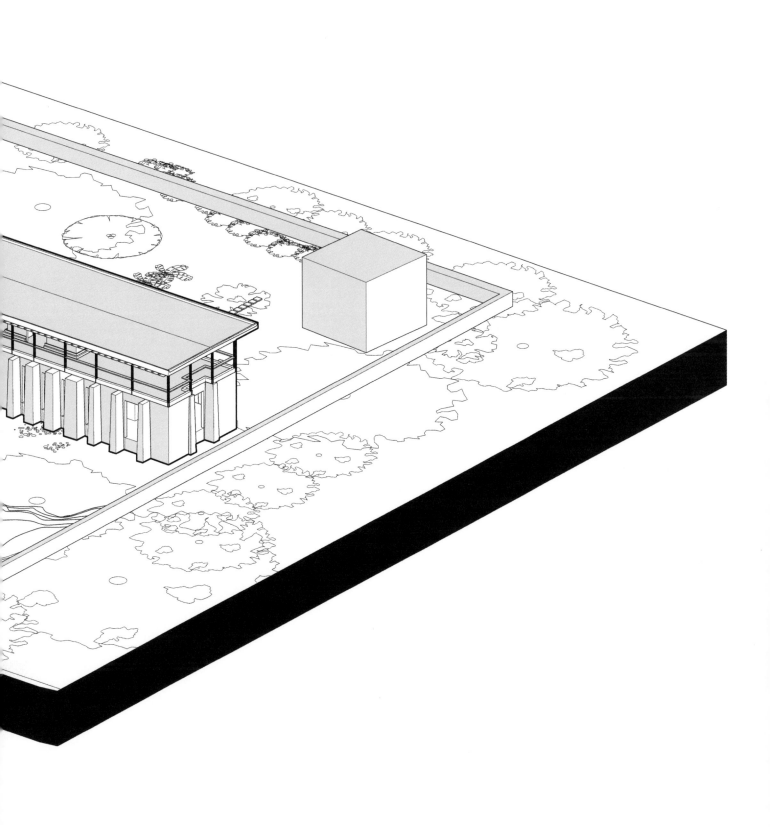

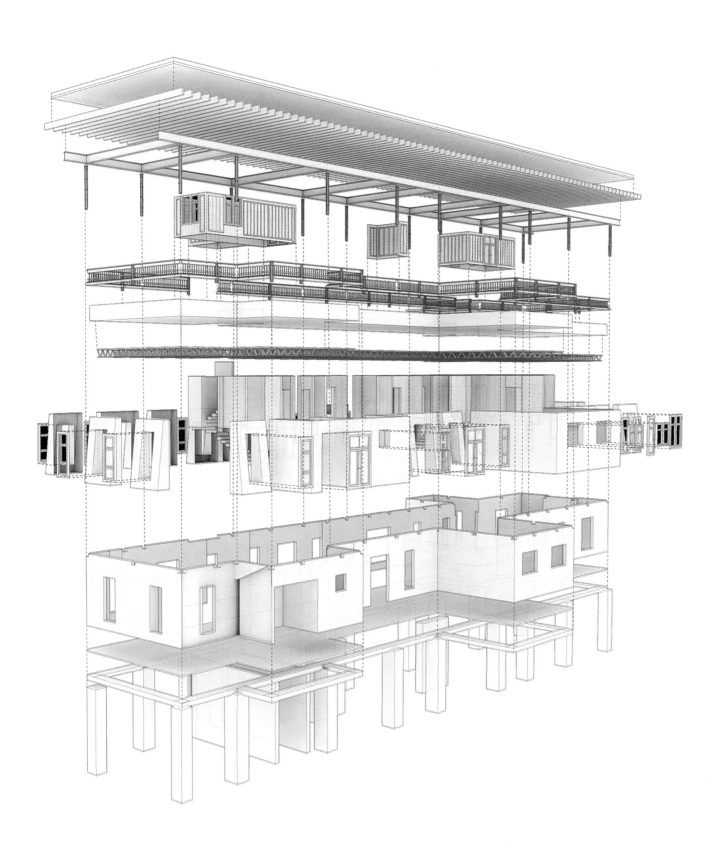

Exploded axonometric

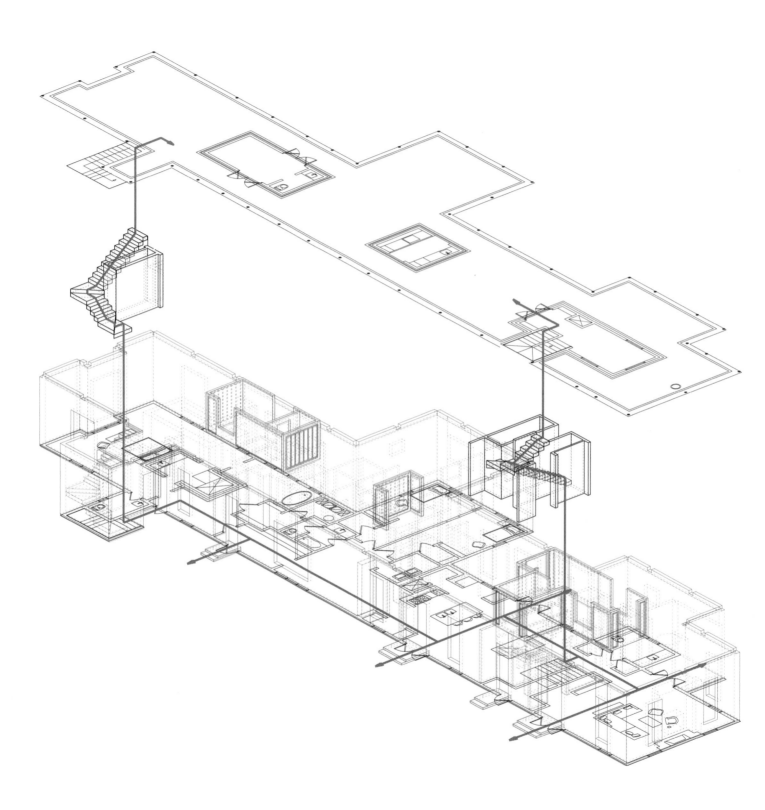

Circulation

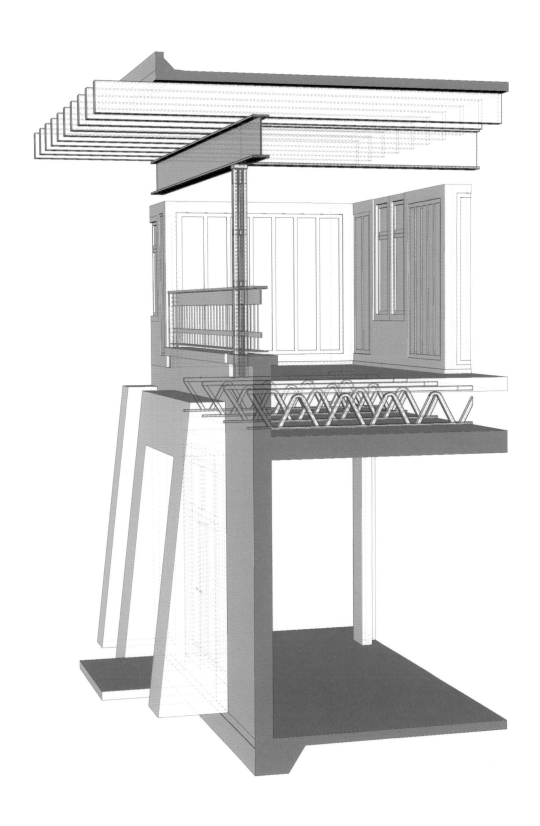

Structural system

3D MODELS

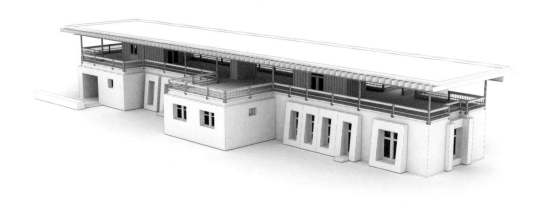

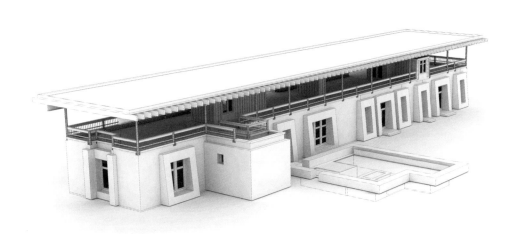

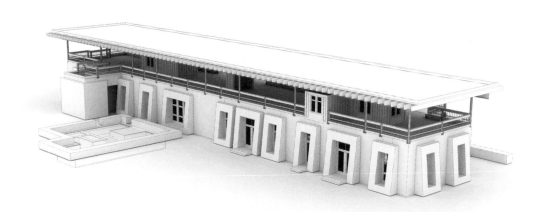

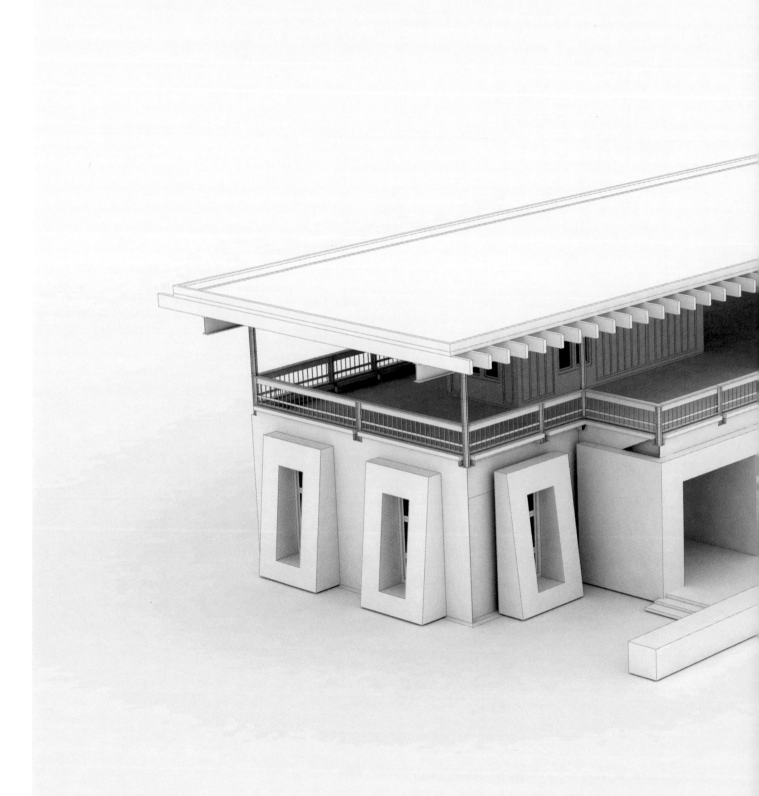

CONSTRUCTION

WORKING DRAWINGS

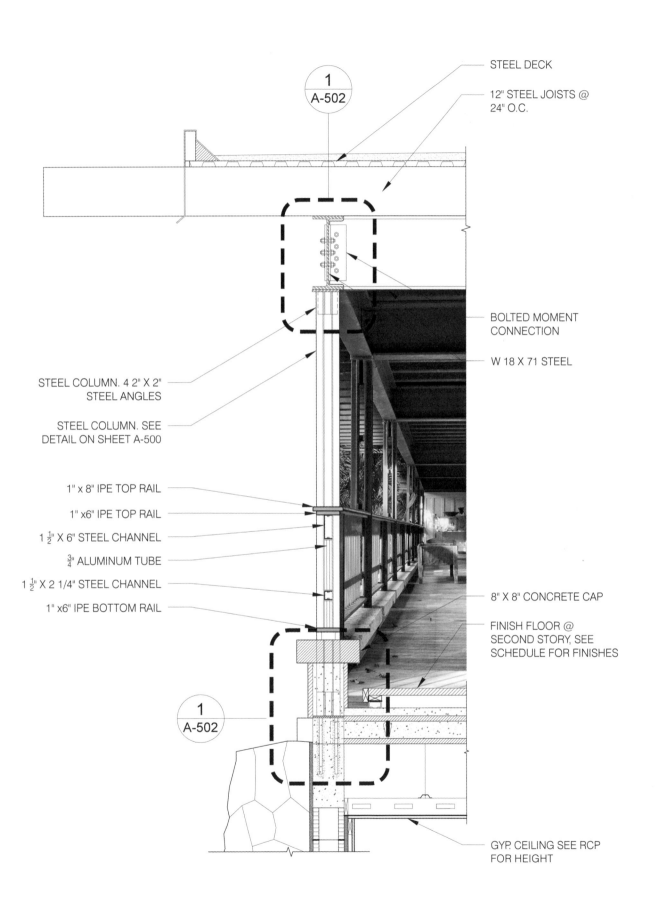

1
A-502

STEEL DECK

12" STEEL JOISTS @
24" O.C.

BOLTED MOMENT
CONNECTION

W 18 X 71 STEEL

STEEL COLUMN. 4 2" X 2"
STEEL ANGLES

STEEL COLUMN. SEE
DETAIL ON SHEET A-500

1" x 8" IPE TOP RAIL

1" x6" IPE TOP RAIL

1 $\frac{1}{2}$" X 6" STEEL CHANNEL

$\frac{3}{4}$" ALUMINUM TUBE

1 $\frac{1}{2}$" X 2 1/4" STEEL CHANNEL

1" x6" IPE BOTTOM RAIL

8" X 8" CONCRETE CAP

FINISH FLOOR @
SECOND STORY, SEE
SCHEDULE FOR FINISHES

1
A-502

GYP. CEILING SEE RCP
FOR HEIGHT

Construction section collage

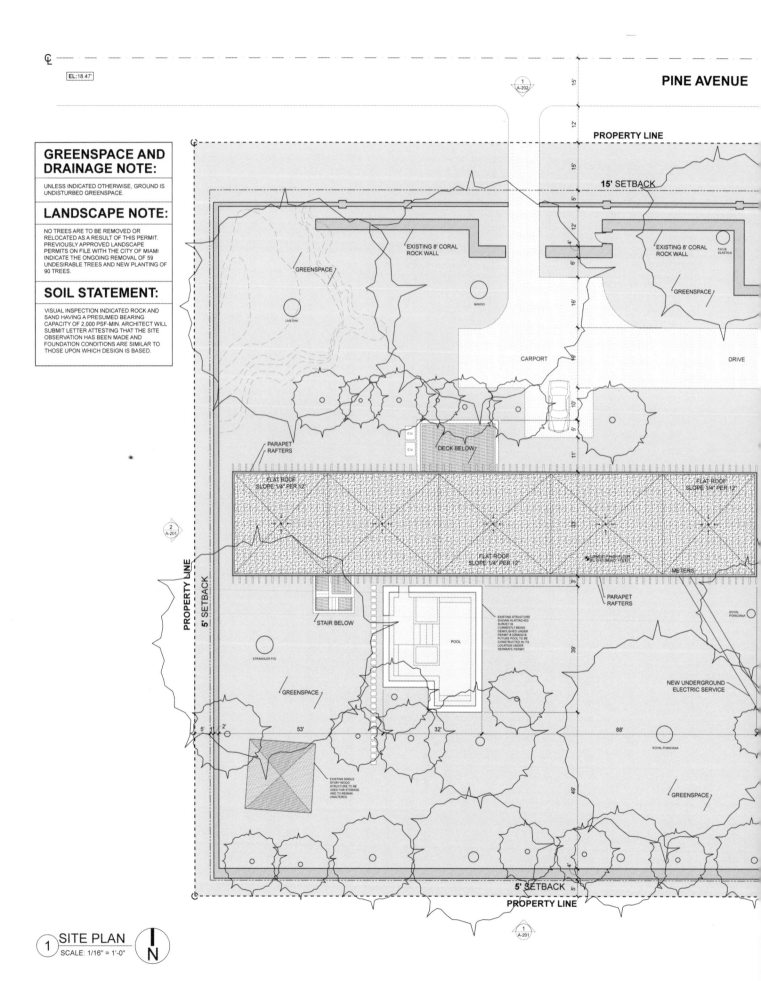

EL:18.47'

PINE AVENUE

PROPERTY LINE

15' SETBACK

GREENSPACE AND DRAINAGE NOTE:

UNLESS INDICATED OTHERWISE, GROUND IS UNDISTURBED GREENSPACE.

LANDSCAPE NOTE:

NO TREES ARE TO BE REMOVED OR RELOCATED AS A RESULT OF THIS PERMIT. PREVIOUSLY APPROVED LANDSCAPE PERMITS ON FILE WITH THE CITY OF MIAMI INDICATE THE ONGOING REMOVAL OF 59 UNDESIRABLE TREES AND NEW PLANTING OF 90 TREES.

SOIL STATEMENT:

VISUAL INSPECTION INDICATED ROCK AND SAND HAVING A PRESUMED BEARING CAPACITY OF 2,000 PSF-MIN. ARCHITECT WILL SUBMIT LETTER ATTESTING THAT THE SITE OBSERVATION HAS BEEN MADE AND FOUNDATION CONDITIONS ARE SIMILAR TO THOSE UPON WHICH DESIGN IS BASED.

GREENSPACE

EXISTING 8' CORAL ROCK WALL

EXISTING 8' CORAL ROCK WALL

FICUS ELASTICA

GREENSPACE

MANGO

LIVE OAK

CARPORT

DRIVE

PARAPET RAFTERS

C.U.

C.U.

DECK BELOW

FLAT ROOF SLOPE 1/4" PER 12"

FLAT ROOF SLOPE 1/4" PER 12"

PROPERTY LINE

5' SETBACK

FLAT ROOF SLOPE 1/4" PER 12"

LOWEST POINT EL 30' BASED

METERS

PARAPET RAFTERS

ROYAL POINCIANA

STAIR BELOW

STRANGLER FIG

POOL

EXISTING STRUCTURE SHOWN IN ATTACHED SURVEY IS CURRENTLY BEING DEMOLISHED UNDER PERMIT #C0500318. FUTURE POOL TO BE CONSTRUCTED IN ITS LOCATION UNDER SEPARATE PERMIT.

GREENSPACE

NEW UNDERGROUND ELECTRIC SERVICE

5' 1' 2'

53'

32'

88'

ROYAL POINCIANA

EXISTING SINGLE STORY WOOD STRUCTURE TO BE USED FOR STORAGE AND TO REMAIN UNALTERED

GREENSPACE

5' SETBACK

PROPERTY LINE

1 SITE PLAN
SCALE: 1/16" = 1'-0"

N

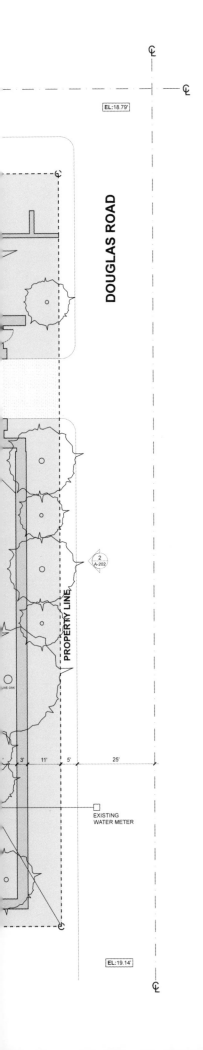

EL:18.79'

DOUGLAS ROAD

2
A-202

PROPERTY LINE

LIVE OAK

3' 11' 5' 25'

EXISTING
WATER METER

EL:19.14'

[STRANG]
ARCHITECTURE

3326 MARY STREET, SUITE 301
COCONUT GROVE, FLORIDA 33133
PH: 305-373-4990 | FX: 305-373-4991
FIRM LICENSE # AA26001123
WWW.STRANGARCHITECTURE.COM

PROJECT LOCATION:
COCONUT GROVE, FL

PROJECT CLIENT(S) / OWNER(S):
MAX AND TAMARA STRANG

ARCHITECT:
MAX WILSON STRANG, RA / AIA
LICENSE # AR0017183
3326 MARY ST #301
MIAMI, FL 33133

STRUCTURAL ENGINEERING:
DIEGO PASERELA

MEP ENGINEERING:
GERRERO GONZOLAS
780 TAMIAM CANAL RD,
MIAMII, FL 33144

GENERAL CONTRACTOR
OXFORD UNIVERSAL
7440 SW 50 TERRACE, SUITE 110,
MIAMI, FL 33155

PROJECT NAME:
ROCKHOUSE

PROFESSIONAL SEAL(S):

No.	DATE	DESCRIPTION

SHEET ISSUE / REVISION LOG

Project ID:	Drawn By:
RH 2004	MAS
Print Date:	Scale:
MAR 03, 2002	AS INDICATED

Sheet Title:

SITE PLAN

Sheet No:

A-100

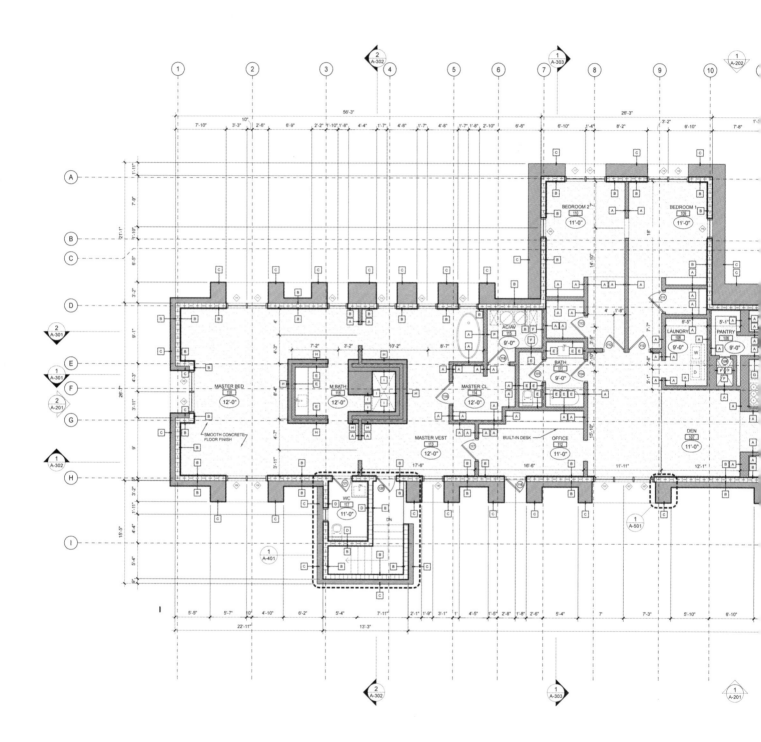

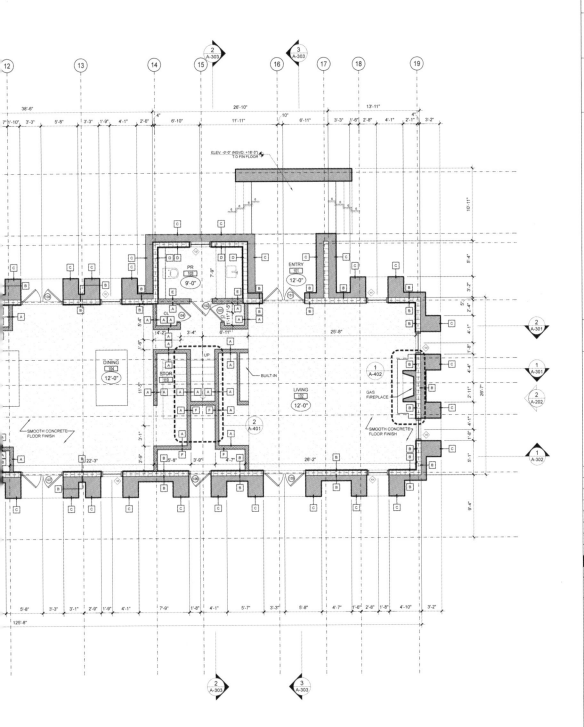

PROJECT LOCATION:
COCONUT GROVE, FL

PROJECT CLIENT(S) / OWNER(S):
MAX AND TAMARA STRANG

ARCHITECT:
MAX WILSON STRANG, RA / AIA
LICENSE # AR0017183
3326 MARY ST #301
MIAMI, FL 33133

STRUCTURAL ENGINEERING:
DIEGO PASERELA

MEP ENGINEERING:
GERRERO GONZOLAS
780 TAMIAM CANAL RD,
MIAMII, FL 33144

GENERAL CONTRACTOR
OXFORD UNIVERSAL
7440 SW 50 TERRACE, SUITE 110,
MIAMI, FL 33155

PROJECT NAME:
ROCKHOUSE

PROFESSIONAL SEAL(S):

No.	DATE	DESCRIPTION

SHEET ISSUE / REVISION LOG

Project ID: RH 2004	Drawn By: MAS
Print Date: MAR 03, 2002	Scale: AS INDICATED

Sheet Title:

FLOOR PLANS

Sheet No:

A-101

FIRST FLOOR PLAN
SCALE: 1/8" = 1'-0"

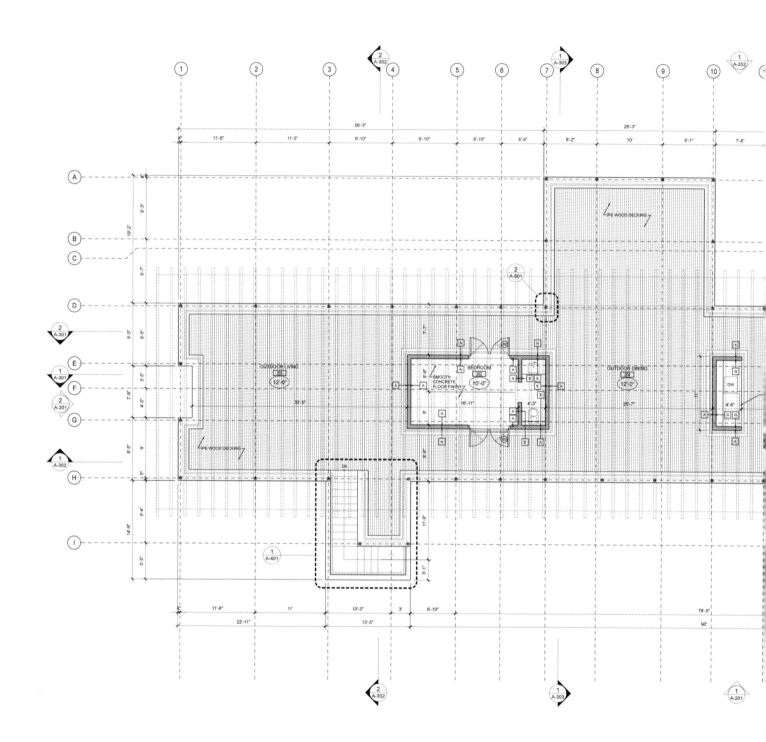

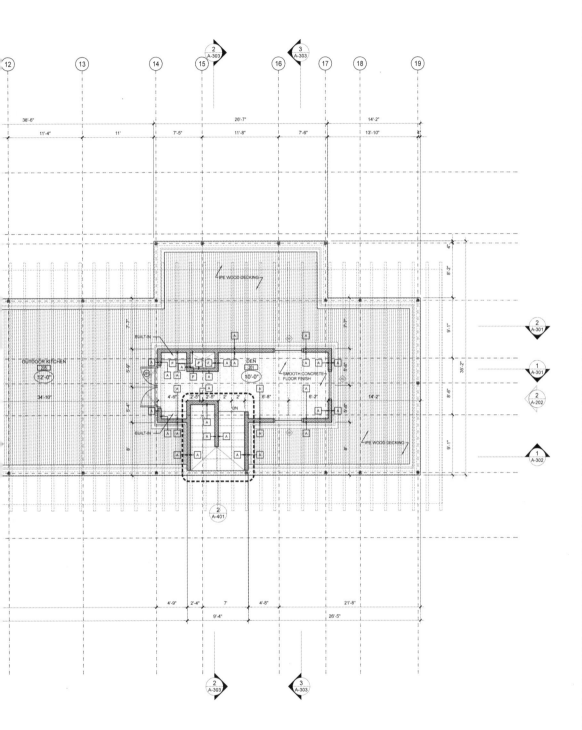

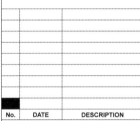

SECOND FLOOR PLAN
SCALE: 1/8" = 1'-0"

N

[STRANG]
ARCHITECTURE

3326 MARY STREET, SUITE 301
COCONUT GROVE, FLORIDA 33133
PH: 305-373-4990 | FX: 305-373-4991
FIRM LICENSE # AA26001123
WWW.STRANGARCHITECTURE.COM

PROJECT LOCATION:
COCONUT GROVE, FL

PROJECT CLIENT(S) / OWNER(S):
MAX AND TAMARA STRANG

ARCHITECT:
MAX WILSON STRANG, RA / AIA
LICENSE # AR0017183
3326 MARY ST #301
MIAMI, FL 33133

STRUCTURAL ENGINEERING:
DIEGO PASERELA

MEP ENGINEERING:
GERRERO GONZOLAS
780 TAMIAM CANAL RD,
MIAMII, FL 33144

GENERAL CONTRACTOR
OXFORD UNIVERSAL
7440 SW 50 TERRACE, SUITE 110,
MIAMI, FL 33155

PROJECT NAME:
ROCKHOUSE

PROFESSIONAL SEAL(S):

No.	DATE	DESCRIPTION

SHEET ISSUE / REVISION LOG

Project ID: **RH 2004**	Drawn By: **MAS**
Print Date: **MAR 03, 2002**	Scale: **AS INDICATED**

Sheet Title:

FLOOR PLANS

Sheet No:

A-102

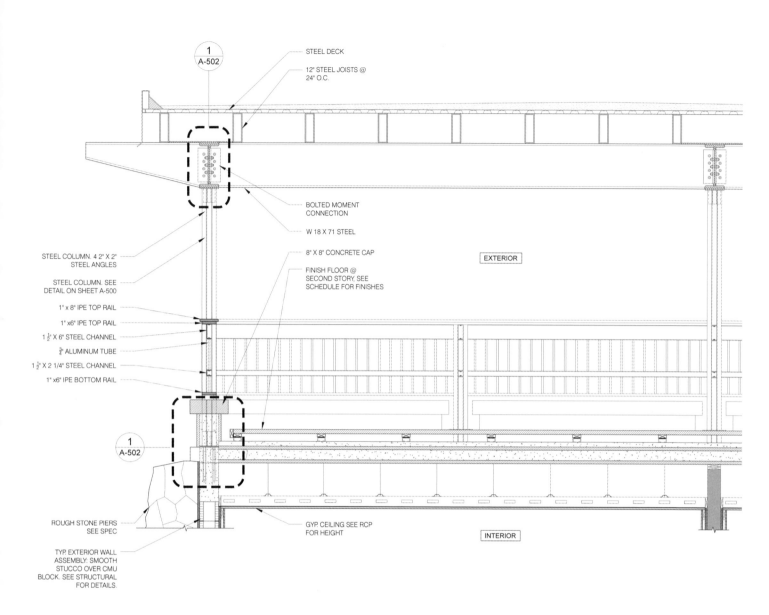

1 / A-502

STEEL DECK

12" STEEL JOISTS @ 24" O.C.

BOLTED MOMENT CONNECTION

W 18 X 71 STEEL

8" X 8" CONCRETE CAP

FINISH FLOOR @ SECOND STORY, SEE SCHEDULE FOR FINISHES

EXTERIOR

STEEL COLUMN. 4 2" X 2" STEEL ANGLES

STEEL COLUMN. SEE DETAIL ON SHEET A-500

1" x 8" IPE TOP RAIL

1" x 6" IPE TOP RAIL

1 1/2" X 6" STEEL CHANNEL

3/4" ALUMINUM TUBE

1 1/2" X 2 1/4" STEEL CHANNEL

1" x 6" IPE BOTTOM RAIL

1 / A-502

ROUGH STONE PIERS SEE SPEC

TYP. EXTERIOR WALL ASSEMBLY: SMOOTH STUCCO OVER CMU BLOCK. SEE STRUCTURAL FOR DETAILS.

GYP. CEILING SEE RCP FOR HEIGHT

INTERIOR

1 WALL SECTION
SCALE: 3/4" = 1'-0"

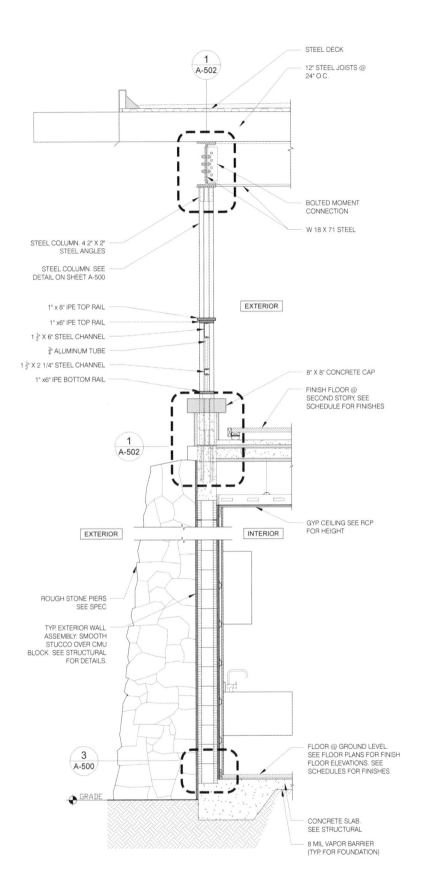

STEEL DECK

12" STEEL JOISTS @
24" O.C.

1
A-502

BOLTED MOMENT
CONNECTION

W 18 X 71 STEEL

STEEL COLUMN. 4 2" X 2"
STEEL ANGLES

STEEL COLUMN. SEE
DETAIL ON SHEET A-500

EXTERIOR

1" x 8" IPE TOP RAIL

1" x 6" IPE TOP RAIL

1 ½" X 6" STEEL CHANNEL

¾" ALUMINUM TUBE

1 ½" X 2 ¼" STEEL CHANNEL

1" x 6" IPE BOTTOM RAIL

8" X 8" CONCRETE CAP

FINISH FLOOR @
SECOND STORY, SEE
SCHEDULE FOR FINISHES

1
A-502

GYP. CEILING SEE RCP
FOR HEIGHT

EXTERIOR

INTERIOR

ROUGH STONE PIERS
SEE SPEC

TYP EXTERIOR WALL
ASSEMBLY: SMOOTH
STUCCO OVER CMU
BLOCK. SEE STRUCTURAL
FOR DETAILS.

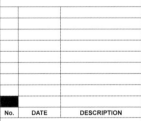

3
A-500

FLOOR @ GROUND LEVEL.
SEE FLOOR PLANS FOR FINISH
FLOOR ELEVATIONS. SEE
SCHEDULES FOR FINISHES

GRADE

CONCRETE SLAB.
SEE STRUCTURAL

8 MIL VAPOR BARRIER
(TYP. FOR FOUNDATION)

2 WALL SECTION
SCALE: 3/4" = 1'-0"

[STRANG]
ARCHITECTURE

3326 MARY STREET, SUITE 301
COCONUT GROVE, FLORIDA 33133
PH: 305-373-4990 | FX: 305-373-4991
FIRM LICENSE # AA26001123
WWW.STRANGARCHITECTURE.COM

PROJECT LOCATION:
COCONUT GROVE, CO

PROJECT CLIENT(S) / OWNER(S):
MAX AND TAMARA STRANG

ARCHITECT:
MAX WILSON STRANG, RA / AIA
LICENSE # AR0017183
3326 MARY ST #301
MIAMI, FL 33133

STRUCTURAL ENGINEERING:
DIEGO PASERELA

MEP ENGINEERING:
GERRERO GONZOLAS
780 TAMIAM CANAL RD,
MIAMII, FL 33144

GENERAL CONTRACTOR
OXFORD UNIVERSAL
7440 SW 50 TERRACE, SUITE 110,
MIAMI, FL 33155

PROJECT NAME:
ROCKHOUSE

PROFESSIONAL SEAL(S):

No.	DATE	DESCRIPTION

SHEET ISSUE / REVISION LOG

Project ID: RH 2004	Drawn By: MAS
Print Date: MAR 03, 2002	Scale: AS INDICATED

Sheet Title:

WALL SECTIONS

Sheet No:

A-400

059

SITE

PROCESS

THE BUILDING

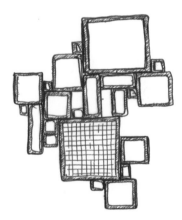

GATE CONCEPT

Film and Television are in the business of imagination. Mise-en-scène are artfully crafted; locations are transported from one side of the world to another. One has only to walk down the streets of downtown Toronto on any given day, past the slates of New York City police cars and camera set-ups to recognize that creative measures are frequently employed with regards to site and locations.

And so it is with the RockHouse. The house's sheer beauty makes it an ideal cinematic back-drop, but, more than that, it's pan-Asian modernity exists in a curiously unattributable universe. It could as easily be located in the jungles of South America as on a small island in the Andaman Sea.

On that note, the RockHouse was used in Michael Mann's major Hollywood film, Miami Vice, as the home of a drug baron and his irrepressibly chic lieutenant, played by Luis Tosar and Gong Li, respectively.

The house's furnishings were customized to provide more of a 'drug-lord' aesthetic, though otherwise remained largely unchanged. However, through the magic of CGI, the entire house was transported to South America, at the edge of a jungle, overlooking cliffs and waterfalls.

The story of how the RockHouse wound up in the film is one of serendipity; worthy of a screen-writer. The original Miami Vice television series, in the 1980s, was instrumental in introducing Miami's inimitable Art Deco chic to a broader audience, and ultimately saved countless buildings, and inspired the Miami Beach Architectural District.

So when a location scout showed up at the door, asking Strang whether he would consider having RockHouse be featured in the film, he happily agreed. Weeks later, he received a call saying that the house had not been selected. Only to be called back the next day by the same scout, saying that Mann had driven past RockHouse en route to another location, stopped the car dead in its tracks, and said simply 'there it is'.

EPILOGUE

BY MAX STRANG

In 1999, while on an afternoon jog through the leafy streets of Coconut Grove, I discovered the site on which the RockHouse would eventually be constructed. The one-acre site had a small two-bedroom cottage which was completely surrounded by an almost impenetrable landscape. I instantly fell in love with the site and its intense treescape which included an impressive Florida Strangler Fig, Royal Poincianas, Royal Palms, Live Oaks, and exuberant stands of giant bamboo. In fact, a tree survey indicated over three hundred trees were jammed onto this one acre parcel. I purchased the property and not long afterwards I moved into the cottage with my soon-to-be wife, Tamara. We lived on the property for several years while we slowly cleared out the invasive trees and began to envision the designs for a new house.

Miami is partially situated upon a ridge of oolitic limestone. Oolite, as it is more commonly known, is the bedrock of Miami and rises to a height of eighteen feet above current sea level. This rock ridge makes itself most evident in Coconut Grove. For all of Miami's short history, architects and builders have been incorporating oolite into their designs. The widespread adoption of this local building material has given Coconut Grove a special sense of place. It was without question that the RockHouse would be built with oolite… and lots of it!

The "parti" for the RockHouse could not be more straightforward: it is a simple stone house protected by a detached roof canopy. Much like Rudolph's Umbrella House of 1953, the RockHouse relies upon its roof canopy to shield it from the intense tropical sun and frequent downpours. However, programmatically it has more in common with Bawa's Villa at Batu Jimbar, as the roof canopy allows for an occupiable, open-air living space.

Clearly, the structural expression of the RockHouse is a derivation of a lifetime to exposure to the work of Leedy and the Sarasota School. It is impossible not to compare its roof canopy to Leedy's Ellison, Dormon, Sands and Solomon Residences. The pre-cast concrete "double-tees" were so pervasive throughout Leedy's entire career that they undoubtedly became a part of my architectural subconscious. Additionally,

one can not escape the simple conclusion that Leedy's Strang Residence (Winter Haven, 1969), in which I was raised, had the most profound effect on me.

In the case of Leedy, the repetition of structural elements became the defining architectural elements of his buildings. Long-spans and cantilevers appealed to Leedy's quest for "bold architecture" while also addressing issues of practicality, economy and efficiency of construction. Structure and shade became synonymous.

In lieu of precast concrete the RockHouse features structural steel columns and joists. However, it's not the choice of material but the repetitive effect of the structural members that continues the lineage of Leedy. It is worth noting that decades earlier, Paul Rudolph also demonstrated the same effect with wood components in his designs of the Harkavy House and Umbrella House in Sarasota.

I had the immense pleasure of living in the RockHouse from 2004 until 2010. Tamara and I raised our children in this house during their years of early childhood. It was pure joy to watch them run amok beneath its steel roof canopy and explore the mini-jungle that surrounded the home. In 2010 we sold the home and relocated to Telluride, Colorado to embark upon an entirely new chapter of our lives. Despite the move to Colorado, the Miami office remained open and has continued to grow. Many new commissions followed the design of the RockHouse, however, no attempts were ever made to replicate its design.

The RockHouse stands as a site-specific and climate-specific design that resonates with its unique site in Coconut Grove (Miami). I am thankful that the new owners of the home are enjoying it's enduring beauty and tropical lifestyle. Over the years, many different photographers have captured various eras of interior design. Outside, the evolving landscape has continued to envelop the home. This book includes countless photos that span fifteen years from construction to ongoing occupancy. Now, through this publication, many more people can enjoy the RockHouse and learn more about its inspirations and architectural design.

APPENDIX

FIRM PROFILE

[STRANG]

The firm has received more AIA design awards for its South Florida homes than any other architect currently practicing in the region. Founded by Max Strang in 1998, the Miami-based firm has since expanded to include addtional offices in Fort Lauderdale and Sarasota. [STRANG] specializes in modern residential design and it's work can be found across Florida, the Florida Keys, the Bahamas, Dominican Republic, Colorado and the United Arab Emirates.

The firm provides integrated design services in the fields of architecture, interior design, lighting design and landscape design for the residential market. This includes new construction residences, condominum residences, boutique hotels and masterplans of residential communities.

Jason Adams serves as the Vice President of the firm and has been instrumental in the operational success of the firm.

Widespread acclaim for the firm includes publications with The New York Times, The Wall Street Journal, Wallpaper* and even Playboy. In 2010, the firm was honored by the Miami chapter of the American Insitute of Architects as its Firm of the Year.

Max Strang FAIA

Max Strang is the founding principal of [STRANG], a Miami-based architecture firm acclaimed for its site-specific and climate-driven designs. Through his work and discourse, Strang has consistently underscored the ongoing relevance and importance of regional modernism to an international audience. In 2016, he was elected to the prestigious College of Fellows of the American Institute of Architects (AIA) and in 2013 he received the Silver Medal from the Miami Chapter of the AIA, the highest honor the organization can bestow.

Strang worked in London for the world-renowned Zaha Hadid and in New York for SHoP Architects. The architect of greatest influence, however, was Florida's Gene Leedy, an important member of the Sarasota School of Architecture. Strang was raised in a Leedy-designed home and later interned in Leedy's Winter Haven office. He graduated summa cum laude with a degree in architecture from the University of Florida and received a graduate degree from Columbia University. As one of Florida's pre-eminent practitioners of regional modernism, Strang has demonstrated that the optimistic spirit of the movement can indeed be advanced into a new era. This continuity of tradition and critical exploration have infused the firm's projects across the state of Florida and the Caribbean.

[STRANG] Team

Max Strang	Founding Principal, *Shareholder*
Jason Adams	Principal, *Shareholder*
Elizabeth Starr	Architectural Director, *Associate*
Alexandra Mangimelli	Architectural Director, *Associate*
Maria Ascoli	Creative Director
Travis Harrison	Landscape Director
Matthew Cohen	Senior Project Architect
Evelyn Alejo	Senior Project Manager
Pedro Rojas	Project Manager
Kathryn Green	Project Manager
Matthew Slingerland	Project Manager
Marcela Arango	Project Manager
Vanessa Arteaga	Interior Designer
Jessica Croitoru	Interior Designer
Blanca Martinez	Designer
Mitchell Clarke	Designer
Philip Elmore	Designer
Andrea Rebull	Designer
Jake Farris	Designer
Luis Espinoza	Designer
Douglas Nassar	Designer
Kalil Mella	Designer
Shirely Deutch	Accounts Manager
Esti Brooks	Office Manager

PROJECT CREDITS

Architect
[STRANG]

Design Team
Max Strang

Interior Design
Max & Tamara Strang (original installations)

Location
Coconut Grove (Miami), Florida, USA

Client
Max & Tamara Strang

Project Year
2001

Completion
2004

Land Area
1 acre

Built Area
8,000 adjusted square feet

Budget
$2,000,00 / square metre

Book Text Editing
Max Strang, Byron Hawes, Oscar Riera Ojeda

Photography
Claudio Manzoni, Claudia Uribe-Touri, Moris Moreno, Hans Fonk, Max Strang

Miami Vice Imagery
Courtesy Universal Pictures

Aerial photography
Courtesy of Rex Hamilton

Construction process photography
Max Strang

General Contractor
Eduardo Fernandes
Oxford Universal Corporation

Structural Engineering
Diego Passarella, P.E.

HVAC Design
Guerrero Gonzalez Engineers Inc.

Aquatic Design
Greenbrook Pools Inc

Geotechnical Engineering
Ardaman & Associates Inc.

Stone Mason (House)
Ranford Stewart & Associates

Stone Mason (Landscape Walls)
David Goodrich, Ryan Dovenberg, Barry Massin & Associates

Structural Steel Fabrication & Assembly
Caballero Iron Works of Florida

Steel Gate Fabrication
Metal Man Inc & Barry Massin

Landscape Consultant
Avalon Gardens
Grandison & Sons Landscaping

Rock Consultant
Barry Massin

Specialty Consultant
Todd Wilson

Photovoltaic System
Hypower Incorporated

Plumbing Subcontractor
Ameritemp Inc

Millwork Subcontractor
Round Tuit Carpentry Inc

Kitchen Installation
Karina Kitchen Kabinets Inc

HVAC
Ameritemp Inc

Wood Supplier
Allwoods Inc.

Dumpsters & Backhoes
Lopefra Corporation

Construction Structural System
Poured Concrete, Hambro Joists, Structural Steel

Cladding
Oolitic Limestone & Florida Keystone

Roofing
Hambro Hybrid Concrete & Joist System

Windows
CGI Impact Resistant

Doors
CGI Impact Resistant

Decking
FSC Certified Ipe

Hardware
Schlage Inc

Bathroom Fixtures
Starck

PHOTOGRAPHY CAPTIONS

View of House from pool.
Photograph by Claudio Manzoni.

Upper Terrace of RockHouse with exposed steel roof system.
Photograph by Claudia Uribe-Touri.

View from upper terrace towards Southern Garden.
Photograph by Max Strang.

The riotous landscape of Coconut Grove envelops the home.
Photograph by The Rex Hamilton Corporation.

Giant banyan trees create a tunnel of green along Main Highway in Coconut Grove.
Photograph by Claudia Uribe-Touri.

Aerial roots of a nearby banyan tree.
Photograph by Max Strang.

Typical street scene in Coconut Grove.
Photograph by Max Strang.

The property features large stands of bambusa vulgaris.
Photograph by Claudio Manzoni.

View of root system of tree on neighboring property.
Photograph by Claudia Uribe-Touri.

Trail through the site.
Photograph by Max Strang.

Site vegetation.
Photograph by Max Strang.

The home is immersed into the tropical landscape of Coconut Grove.
Photograph by Claudio Manzoni.

An original wood-frame cottage at the jobsite where Max Strang's family lived prior to the construction of the RockHouse.
Photograph by Max Strang.

Foundations of original wood-framed home were incorporated into the design of the swimming pool.
Photograph by Max Strang.

Max Strang standing within the edge of the building footprint.
Photograph by Tamara Strang.

Ryan Dovenberg, David Goodrich and Max Strang during construction of perimeter wall.
Photograph by Tamara Strang.

Max & Tamara Strang with dog Mango.
Photograph by Strang Architecture.

Royal Palm being relocated onsite.
Photograph by Max Strang.

Relocation of a Royal palm prior to
the house construction.
Photograph by Max Strang.

Delivery of "oolite" from a nearby
excavation site.
Photograph by Tamara Strang.

Oolite boulders are incorporated into
the perimeter wall construction.
Photograph by Max Strang.

Custom steel gate designed in
conjunction with Barry Massin.
Photograph by Max Strang.

Ryan Dovenberg building the
perimeter site wall with oolitic
limestone rocks.
Photograph by Max Strang.

Concrete slab with steel reinforcing.
Photograph by Max Strang.

Pumping concrete to the far-
reaches of the jobsite.
Photograph by Max Strang.

Custom steel columns are embedded
into a perimeter concrete beam.
Photograph by Max Strang.

Tamara Strang during early stages
of steel roof installation.
Photograph by Max Strang.

Interior staircase are constructed with
poured-in-place concrete.
Photograph by Max Strang.

Interior of future kitchen.
Photograph by Max Strang.

The steel roof is taking shape.
Photograph by Max Strang.

Steel columns and beams are
positioned into place.
Photograph by Max Strang.

Large oolite boulders will be used as
landscape features.
Photograph by Max Strang.

Steel roof assembly completed.
Photograph by Max Strang.

Corrugated metal decking is supported by the steel roof joists.
Photograph by Max Stang.

Ranford Stewart and associate applying "oolite" to the exterior of the house wall.
Photograph by Max Strang.

Liquid applied waterproofing membrane is being applied to the second-floor, concrete slab.
Photograph by Max Strang.

Oolitic limestone application at the exterior staircase.
Photograph by Max Strang.

Installation of "thin film" solar photovoltaic system underway.
Photograph by Max Strang.

View from driveway towards north elevation of house.
Photograph by Claudio Manzoni.

View from entry driveway towards front door.
Photograph by Claudio Manzoni.

Oolitic limestone rocks serve as a powerful 'base' for the architectural assemblage.
Photograph by Max Strang.

View from garden towards north elevation of house.
Photograph by Claudio Manzoni.

North side of house at dusk.
Photograph by RSG TEAM.

Path leading to kitchen entrance.
Photograph by Claudio Manzoni.

Outdoor pathway leading to kitchen entrance.
Photograph by Claudio Manzoni.

The rust finish of the steel roof glows above the second floor open terrace.
Photograph by Claudio Manzoni.

Ficus aurea (Florida Strangler Fig) in foreground immediately outside of master bedrooom.
Photograph by Claudio Manzoni.

Pathway along south side of house.
Photograph by Claudio Manzoni.

Monumental Oolite pillars frame each opening.
Photograph by Claudio Manzoni.

Secondary entrance to home through kitchen.
Photograph by Claudio Manzoni.

View from garden towards Kitchen.
Photograph by Claudio Manzoni.

Oolitic limestone and roots of Florida Strangler Fig.
Photograph by Max Strang.

Front entrance.
Photograph by Claudio Manzoni.

East Timor doors purchased by Tamara and Max Strang on a trip to Bali.
Photograph by Max Strang.

Front entrance detail.
Photograph by Claudio Manzoni.

View from garden into Living Room.
Photograph by Claudio Manzoni.

Current furniture arrangement in living room.
Photograph by Claudio Manzoni.

Living room view with original furniture arrangement.
Photograph by Moris Moreno.

Living room.
Photograph by Hans Fonk.

Living room night view.
Photograph by Max Strang.

Hallway toward master bedroom.
Photograph by Moris Moreno.

Living room with original classic modern furniture.
Photograph by Laurent de Verneuil.

Balinese console table with "Moonrise" photograph by Clyde Butcher.
Photograph by Claudia Uribe-Touri.

Current furniture layout of kitchen and lounge.
Photograph by Claudio Manzoni.

Original furniture layout of kitchen and dinnig area.
Photograph by Moris Moreno.

Current furniture layout of kitchen and lounge.
Photograph by Hans Fonk.

Tamara Strang and Lopefra in the kitchen.
Photograph by Claudia Uribe-Touri.

Master bedroom with original furniture arrangement.
Photograph by Hans Fonk.

Current furniture arrangement in master bedroom.
Photograph by RSG TEAM.

Master bedroom with original furniture arrangement.
Photograph by Claudia Uribe-Touri.

Alternative furniture layout in master bedroom.
Photograph by Moris Moreno.

View from master bedroom of Florida Strangler Fig and historical cottage beyond.
Photograph by Claudio Manzoni.

Secondary bedroom.
Photograph by RSG TEAM.

Secondary bedroom.
Photograph by RSG TEAM.

Powder room.
Photograph by Moris Moreno.

Master bathroom suite.
Photograph by Moris Moreno.

Master bathroom suite.
Photograph by RSG TEAM.

Interior stairs.
Photograph by Claudio Manzoni.

Interior stairs.
Photograph by Claudio Manzoni.

View from hall into living room.
Photograph by Claudio Manzoni.

Upper floor lounge.
Photograph by Claudio Manzoni.

Stone statue purchased by
Tamara and Max Strang on a
trip to Bali.
Photograph by Max Strang.

Syd Solomon artwork in upper
floor lounge.
Photograph by Max Strang.

Upper floor lounge.
Photograph by Max Strang.

Tropical atmosphere of upper terrace.
Photograph by Claudio Manzoni.

Tropical atmosphere of upper terrace.
Photograph by Claudio Manzoni.

Upper terrace corridor.
Photograph by Claudio Manzoni.

Guest bedroom on upper terrace.
Photograph by Claudio Manzoni.

Guest bedroom on upper terrace.
Photograph by RSG TEAM.

Rust patina on upper terrace
steelwork exposed roof.
Photograph by Max Strang.

Upper terrace detail.
Photograph by Max Strang.

Rust patina on upper terrace
steelwork.
Photograph by Max Strang.

Rust patina on upper terrace
steelwork.
Photograph by Claudio Manzoni.

Upstairs guest bedroom.
Photograph by Claudio Manzoni.

Palm vases from Bali.
Photograph by Max Strang.

Upper terrace outdoor lounge.
Photograph by Robin Hill.

Upper terrace dinning area.
Photograph by RSG TEAM.

Upper terrace kitchen area.
Photograph by RSG TEAM.

Upper terrace outdoor lounge.
Photograph by Claudia Uribe-Touri.

Upper terrace view.
Photograph by Claudio Manzoni.

Detail of guardrails.
Photograph by Claudio Manzoni.

Keystone stonework around
a wall edge.
Photograph by Claudio Manzoni.

Detail of guardrail and stone base.
Photograph by Claudio Manzoni,

View from upper deck.
Photograph by Claudio Manzoni.

Panoramic photograph of
upper terrace.
Photograph by Max Strang.

Ian Strang on the upper deck.
Photograph by Moris Moreno.

Intersection of guardrail and
structural steel column.
Photograph by Claudio Manzoni.

Detail of guardrail.
Photograph by Claudio Manzoni.

Plant growth on upstairs keystone.
Photograph by Max Strang.

Wood deck and guardrail of
upper terrace.
Photograph by Claudio Manzoni.

Detail of upstairs terrace.
Photograph by Caludio Manzoni.

Detail of upstairs terrace.
Photograph by Claudio Manzoni.

Natural patina of Florida keystone.
Photograph by Claudio Manzoni.

Assemblage of stone and steel.
Photograph by Max Strang.

Aluminum and steel components
of guardrail.
Photograph by Max Strang.

Detail of custom steel columns.
Photograph by Claudio Manzoni.

View from upper terrace towards
southern garden.
Photograph by Robin Hill.

Dining terrace on upper deck.
Photograph by Claudia Uribe-Touri.

Western portion of RockHouse slips
below a massive Strangler Fig.
Photograph by Max Strang.

Lounge area adjacent to house.
Photograph by Claudio Manzoni.

View of house from pool.
Photograph by RSG TEAM.

Pool area.
Photograph by RSG TEAM.

The zig-zag pool.
Photograph by Claudia Uribe-Touri.

View of RockHouse pool and
southern garden.
Photograph by Claudio Manzoni.

Swimming pool was built among
the ruins of the old cottage.
Photograph by Claudia Uribe-Touri.

Upper terrace lounge at east end.
Photograph by Claudio Manzoni.

Tropical atmosphere of RockHouse.
Photograph by Claudio Manzoni.

Pathway adjacent to pool.
Photograph by Max Strang.

Secluded lounge built adjacent to ruins of old cottage.
Photograph by Claudio Manzoni.

Outdoor dining area.
Photograph by RSG TEAM.

Royal palms frame the massive Florida Strangler Fig in the distance.
Photograph by Max Strang.

South elevation of RockHouse.
Photograph by Claudio Manzoni.

Southern garden and fire pit of RockHouse.
Photograph by RSG TEAM.

Southern garden.
Photograph by RSG TEAM.

Pedestrian gate on Douglas Road.
Photograph by Claudia Uribe-Touri.

Detail of pedestrian gate on Douglas Road.
Photograph by Claudia Uribe-Touri.

Detail of pedestrian gate on Douglas Road.
Photograph by Claudia Uribe-Touri.

Night view of pool.
Photograph by RSG TEAM.

RockHouse at dusk.
Photograph by RSG TEAM.

The RockHouse was digitally reconstructed adjacent to the Iguazú Falls for Miami Vice.
Photograph by Universal Pictures.

Actress Gong Li on set during Miami Vice filming.
Photograph by Universal Pictures.

Miami Vice filming.
Photograph by Max Strang.

Miami Vice filming.
Photograph by Max Strang.

Miami Vice filming.
Photograph by Max Strang.

Miami Vice filming.
Photograph by Max Strang.

Strang family during the filming of Miami Vice.
Photograph by Gary Sisler.

Max & Tamara Strang on the set of Miami Vice.
Photograph by Gary Sisler.

Luis Tosar and Gong Li on the upper terrace of the RockHouse during filming of Miami Vice.
Photograph by Universal Pictures.

A new bedroom suite was constructed on the upper terrace for the filming of Miami Vice.
Photograph by Universal Pictures.

Still frame from Miami Vice with actress Gong Li.
Photograph by Universal Pictures.

Still frame from Miami Vice.
Photograph by Universal Pictures.

Still frame from Miami Vice with actor Luis Tosar.
Photograph by Universal Pictures.

South American druglord portrayed by Luis Tosar during the filming of Miami Vice.
Photograph by Universal Pictures.

South American druglord portrayed by Luis Tosar during the filming of Miami Vice.
Photograph by Universal Pictures.

Max and Tamara Strang with daughter, Emmie, on upper terrace.
Photograph by Claudia Uribe-Touri.

Lopefra on upper terrace after a storm.
Photograph by Max Strang.

Max Strang during an interview on the upper terrace.
Photograph by Jason Adams.

Ian Strang on the upper terrace.
Photograph by Max Strang.

Ian Strang riding a tricycle on the upper terrace.
Photograph by Max Strang.

Emmie Strang during the Miami Vice filming.
Photograph by Max Strang.

Ian and Emmie Strang on the
upper terrace.
Photograph by Max Strang.

Emmie Strang on the upper terrace.
Photograph by Max Strang.

Ian Strang on the upper terrace.
Photograph by Max Strang.

RockHouse north side.
Photograph by Max Strang.

BOOK CREDITS

Book Layout by Oscar Riera Ojeda

OSCAR RIERA OJEDA
PUBLISHERS

Copyright © 2017 by Oscar Riera Ojeda Publishers Limited
ISBN 978-1-946226-07-5
Published by Oscar Riera Ojeda Publishers Limited
Printed in China

Oscar Riera Ojeda Publishers Limited
Unit 4-6, 7/F.,
Far East Consortium Building,
121 Des Voeux Road Central, Hong Kong
T: +852-5311-1625

Production Offices | China
Suit 19, Shenyun Road,
Nanshan District, Shenzhen 518055
T:+86-182-0098-3774

www.oropublishers.com | www.oscarrieraojeda.com
oscar@oscarrieraojeda.com